D1685433

to

from

Text by Lois Rock
Illustrations copyright © 2003 Alex Ayliffe
This edition copyright © 2011 Lion Hudson

The moral rights of the author and illustrator have been asserted

A Lion Children's Book
an imprint of
Lion Hudson plc
Wilkinson House,
Jordan Hill Road,
Oxford OX2 8DR, England
www.lionhudson.com
ISBN: 978 0 7459 6186 6

First edition 2003
This edition 2011
10 9 8 7 6 5 4 3 2 1 0

A catalogue record for this book is available
from the British Library

Typeset in 22/30 Baskerville BT
Printed in China September 2011
(manufacturer LH06)

my very first
Bible

Words by
Lois Rock

Pictures by
Alex Ayliffe

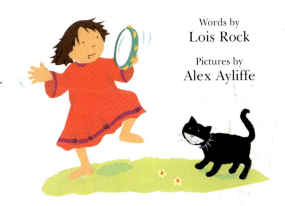

LION
CHILDREN'S

Contents

Old Testament

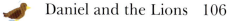

New Testament

Dear God,
These are Bible stories.
Help me to listen.

Dear God,
These are Bible stories.
Help me to imagine.

Dear God,
These are Bible stories.
Help me to understand.

Old Testament

In the Beginning

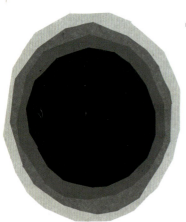

Think of the dark.
Make it darker.
Think of the
darkest dark.

In the beginning,
there was nothing
but dark.

Then God spoke:
"Let there be light."

And the very first light shone
brightly.

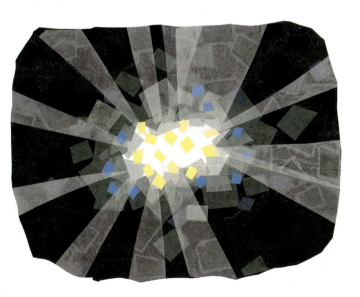

God spread the sky wide above the ocean, and folded the land to make hills and valleys.

God covered the earth with plants: grasses and flowers, vegetables and trees.

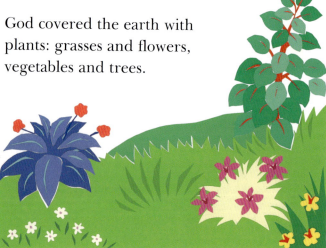

The sun shone in the daytime, and the moon and stars waited for their turn in the night-time.

God made all the creatures.

Birds flew in the sky.

Fish swam in the seas.

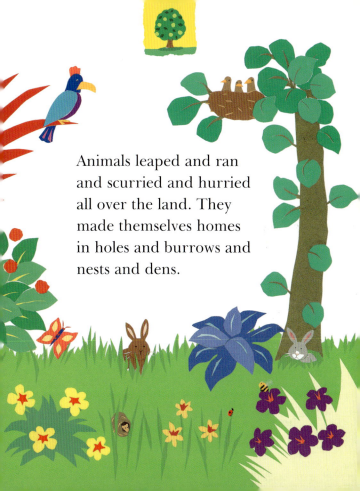

Animals leaped and ran and scurried and hurried all over the land. They made themselves homes in holes and burrows and nests and dens.

Then God made people—man and woman. "Welcome," said God. "You are my friends, and I want you to be safe and happy. Take care of the good world I have made for you.

"Never choose to know about bad things: they will only make you sad."

Everything was perfect...

Then, one day, people wanted to find out about bad things as well as good things.

The snake whispered what to do: they ate some fruit God had told them not to eat.

Their world changed.

They were no longer good friends with God.

Instead, they felt all alone in an unkind world. They had to work very hard for everything they needed.

"Can things ever be put right again?" they wondered. People have been wondering ever since.

Noah and
the Ark

Long ago, God
looked down to
see the world.

God had made
a good world.
Now people
were spoiling it.

They were always fighting.

"I'm sorry I ever made the world," said God. "I shall wash it away."

God saw that there was one good man: Noah.

"I want you to build a big boat," said God to Noah. "It will be called the ark."

Noah was puzzled.

"There is going to be a flood," said God. "You must take your family on the ark, to keep them safe."

Noah began to build.

God said, "Noah, you must also take animals onto the ark. You must take a father and a mother of every kind of animal."

Noah and his family were
very busy doing as God
wanted.

Then it rained and rained.
The whole world was flooded.

The ark floated on the flood
water for days and days and
days.

At last, the rain stopped. The water started to go down.

Bump! Noah's ark hit the top of a mountain and got stuck there.

Noah let out a raven. It flew and flew and kept on flying.

Noah let out a dove.
The first time, it soon
flew back.

The second time, it came
back with an olive branch
in its beak. The third time,
it flew away.

"It must have found land,"
said Noah.

Soon the land was dry.
Noah let everyone out
of the ark. The animals
hurried away to make
new homes.

"Thank you, God, for keeping
us safe," said Noah.

God was pleased. "Look," said God,
"there is my rainbow in the sky.
It is a promise that I will
keep the whole world
safe forever."

Grandfather Abraham

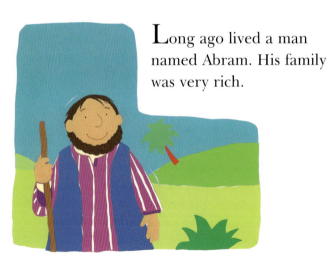

Long ago lived a man named Abram. His family was very rich.

They had sheep and goats
and cattle and donkeys
and camels.

One day, God
spoke to Abram.

"Abram, I want you to leave your father's home and go to a new land.

"I have chosen you to be the great-great-great-grandfather of many people. You and your family will bring my blessing to all the world."

Abram believed that what God
said was true. He set out at
once with his wife, Sarai, his
family and his animals.

They reached the land
of Canaan. "You can make
your home here," said God.

It was a good land, but Abram
had to find grass for his
animals.

They had to keep on moving from place to place. Life was often hard. Sometimes it made them sad.

"I wonder if what God said is really true," thought Abram.

One dark night, God spoke to Abram again. "Look up at the stars in the sky… too many to count," said God. "You will be the great-great-great-grandfather of many people… too many to count."

Abram believed that what God said was true.

"I am going to give you and Sarai new names," said God. "You will be Abraham: Great-great-great-grandfather Abraham.

"Your wife will be Sarah: Great-great-great-grandmother Sarah."

Many years passed. Abraham
and Sarah still had no children.

Abraham sighed. "Can I still
believe that what God said will
come true?" he said.

Sarah looked at other people's children and sighed. "I find it hard to believe that what God said is true," she said.

Then, at last, Sarah and Abraham had a baby. They called him Isaac.

"God has made me so happy I can laugh again," said Sarah. And she knew that one day she was going to be the great-great-great-grandmother of many people.

"This is a time to be happy,"
said Abraham. "Now we
know that what God says
is true."

He was sure that one day
he was going to be the great-
great-great-grandfather of
many people.

Joseph and His Dream

Joseph was wearing his very best coat. He was feeling proud.

His great-grandfather was Abraham.

His grandfather was Isaac.

His father was Jacob.

Jacob had given Joseph the wonderful coat.
It was better than anything he had given to
Joseph's older brothers.

Joseph believed he was very, very important.

His older brothers were very, very jealous.

One day, the brothers were out looking after their father's goats and sheep. Jacob sent Joseph to check that everything was all right.

The brothers grabbed him. They took his coat. Then they saw some merchants passing nearby. They sold Joseph to the men.

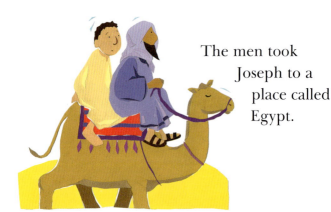

The men took Joseph to a place called Egypt.

The brothers told their father, Jacob, that
Joseph was dead. Jacob was very sad.

In Egypt, Joseph was sold
as a slave. He had to work
very hard. Then someone
told a lie about Joseph and
he went to prison.

Nobody there cared
about Joseph. But
God helped Joseph
understand dreams
and explain their
meaning.

One day, the great king of
Egypt had a strange dream.
Someone sent for Joseph.

Joseph understood the king's dream:

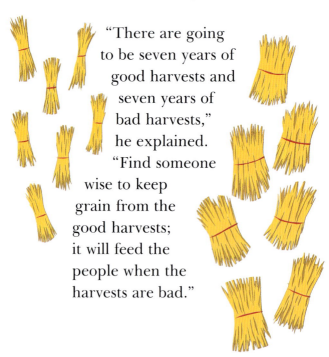

"There are going
to be seven years of
good harvests and
seven years of
bad harvests,"
he explained.
"Find someone
wise to keep
grain from the
good harvests;
it will feed the
people when the
harvests are bad."

The king chose Joseph.
He became very rich and
very important.

The bad years came. Joseph was in
charge of using the grain in the barns.

From far away came ten hungry
people.

They bowed down to the important
man in charge and asked to buy food.

Joseph knew these people
were his brothers, but they
didn't know who he was.

Was Joseph going to
punish them, or was he
going to be kind?

Joseph really wanted to see his one younger brother, Benjamin. He made the others go to fetch him.

Then, at last, Joseph told the brothers who he was. "God was in charge of everything that happened," he said. "I was sent to Egypt so that I could rescue you now."

Joseph invited all his family
to come and live in Egypt.
There they made their home.

Moses and the King

When Miriam was a little girl, she liked to dance and play the tambourine. She also liked to listen to stories with her little brother, Aaron.

They liked the story of Great-great-ever-so-many-greats Grandfather Abraham.

"God promised Abraham a land of our own," said Miriam's mother. "Our family came to Egypt many years ago to find food here. Now the king of Egypt has made us slaves.

"Now the king wants our baby boys killed," she sobbed.

"What about my new baby brother?" Miriam asked.

They hid him in a basket among the reeds.

Miriam saw the princess of Egypt
come and find the baby.

"I shall keep him safe," said the
princess. "I shall call him Moses.
But who will take care of him?"

Miriam stepped forward. "I can find
someone to take care of the baby," she
said. She fetched her mother.

When he was older Moses grew up as a prince, but he knew he was one of the slave people.

One day, he got into a bad fight for trying to help a slave, and he had to run away.

He became a shepherd.

In the desert, Moses saw a strange thing: a bush on fire that wasn't burning. He heard God speaking: "Go back to Egypt, Moses, and tell that king to let my people go. Your brother will help you."

Together Moses and Aaron
went to see the king.

"I will not let your
people go," he told
them.

They asked over and over again, but the king always said, "NO!"

"God wants you to let our people go," said Aaron and Moses. "If you don't, there will be trouble."

There was lots of
trouble: frogs, then
flies, then locusts—
everywhere!

There were all sorts
of horrible things.

At last, the king told Moses and
Aaron to come and see him.
"Hurry up and go!" he said.

God helped everyone escape.
They set out for the land God had
promised to Great-great-ever-so-
many-greats Grandfather Abraham.

Moses and Aaron led the way.

Miriam played her tambourine and danced, just like she used to when she was little.

Brave Joshua

When the way ahead is scary,
who goes first?

Someone who is
strong and brave.

Someone like Joshua.

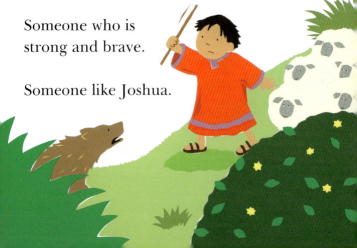

As Moses led his people to
the land God had promised
them, he noticed Joshua.

As Moses told the people God's
laws, he noticed that Joshua
always listened.

"You must love God most of all,
and you must love others as
you love yourself," said Moses.

Joshua always obeyed and tried
to help others to do the same.

The people wandered for
many years on the way to the
new land. Moses grew old.

He chose Joshua to lead the
people into the new land.
Joshua stood on the bank
of the River Jordan, on the
edge of the new land.

"Teach the people to obey my laws," said God, "and I will help you make the land your home."

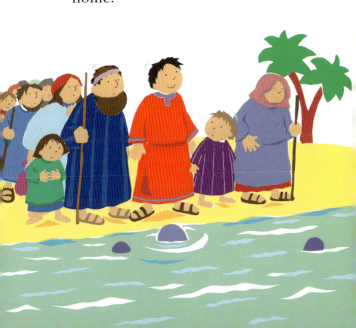

The first place the people came to was the city
of Jericho. It had walls all around it. Strong
soldiers stood on guard.

God told Joshua what to do.

Joshua told the people to march around the city. One day they marched. Two days they marched. Three days they marched. Four days they marched. Five days they marched. Six days they marched. Seven days they marched, and then…

The priests blew
their trumpets.

All the people
shouted.

The walls of
Jericho fell down.

The people entered the city.

It was the first step towards
making the land a home.

When the land was theirs,
Joshua made sure that
everyone had a share.

Then he asked everyone to come to
a great meeting.

"We are at home in the land God has
given us," he said. "I have decided
that I will always live as God wants:
I will love God most of all,
and I will love others as
much as I love myself.
What will you do?"

"We will live as
God wants,"
said the
people.

David and His Song

When he was very little, David liked to throw stones.

When he was bigger, he learned to throw them with a sling.

He was good
at throwing—he
could hit what
he wanted.

At night, his mother told him
about God.

She taught him to say
thank-you prayers to God
for everything he had
and for all the things
he could do.

When David was a bit older, his job was looking after the sheep.

He threw stones to scare away wild animals.

David was never scared. He sang
thank-you songs to God for
everything he had and
for all the things he
could do.

One day, David went to visit his big brothers. They were soldiers.

They were fighting fierce enemies.

One was a giant. He wore shiny battle clothes and had a big spear. "I am Goliath," roared the giant. "If anyone can beat me, then my army will go away! Who dares to try?"

"I dare," said David. For David
believed that God was always
with him and would help
him win.

"You're too little,"
said his brothers.

"You're too little,"
said his king.

"But I can fight lions and
bears and wolves, and I know
God is with me," said David.

"Take care," they warned.

David went out.

He picked up
five stones.

"How dare you fight
me like that!" said the
giant.

"I dare because God is with me,"
said David. He put a stone in his
sling.

He threw.

The giant fell.

David grew up to be the next king of his people. He still sang thank-you songs to God for everything he had and for all he could do.

"Dear God, you are my shepherd,
You give me all I need—
My food, my drink, a place to rest,
Yes, you are good indeed.

When all the world seems gloomy
And scary things are near,
You always take good care of me
And so I need not fear.

You've given me so many things,
And everyone can see
The special loving kindness
You always show to me."

Jonah and the Whale

Jonah was feeling grumpy.

"I'm a prophet," he was thinking. "My job is to tell our people about our God—the God who loves us.

"Now God wants me to go and visit our worst enemies—our enemies in Nineveh. And why?

"BECAUSE GOD WANTS TO
FORGIVE THEM FOR ALL
THE BAD THINGS THEY DO!

"Well, I won't."

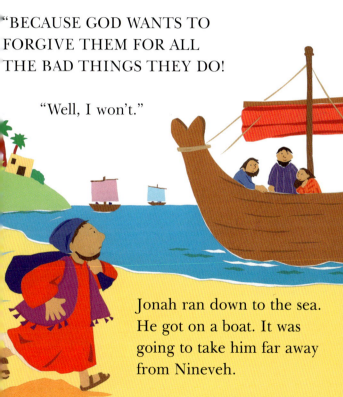

Jonah ran down to the sea.
He got on a boat. It was
going to take him far away
from Nineveh.

Then God sent a storm.

"It's all my fault," wailed Jonah to the sailors. "Throw me overboard, or the storm will sink us all." So they did.

The storm stopped. The sailors on the boat were safe.

Jonah sank deep down in the sea, where a great big fish came and swallowed him up.

Jonah knew that God had
sent the fish.

"Help me, help me!" he
prayed.

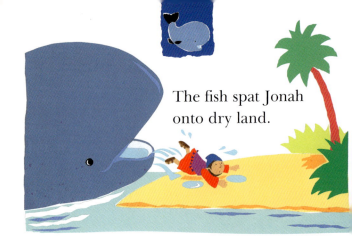

The fish spat Jonah onto dry land.

Once again God told Jonah to go to Nineveh. At last he went.

"Here is a message from God!" he cried. "Stop doing bad things. If you don't, terrible things will happen."

The king heard the news.

"Everyone, stop being bad," he ordered.

God forgave everyone. That made Jonah very grumpy indeed.

He went and made himself a little
shelter. He sat in it and sulked.

"Why are you cross?" asked God.

"The people of Nineveh did bad
things," said Jonah. "You shouldn't
have been kind to them."

God made a lovely plant
grow over Jonah's shelter.

It gave cool shade.

The next day, God sent a worm to eat the plant, and it died.

The sun was hot. The wind was hotter. Jonah was grumpier than ever.

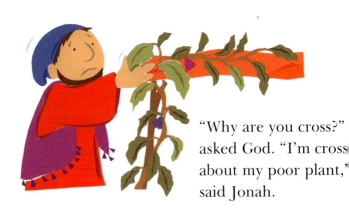

"Why are you cross?" asked God. "I'm cross about my poor plant," said Jonah.

"Are you feeling sorry for a plant?"
said God. "Well, I'm feeling sorry for
all the people of Nineveh and all their
animals. Even if they were once bad,
I still love them."

Daniel and
the Lions

Daniel always did what
he believed was right.

He always said prayers
to God.

He always obeyed God.

Daniel did what he believed was right even when everything else went wrong.

One sad day, the great-great-great-ever-so-many-great-grandchildren of Abraham lost a fight against enemy soldiers.

Daniel was one of the people taken far away. He went to Babylon.

Everything was going wrong.

Daniel went on doing what
he believed was right.

He always followed God's laws.

The king of Babylon saw that
Daniel was a good man. He gave
him a very important job.

That made other
people very jealous.

They went to see the king.

"O king," they said. "You are so great and wonderful. Make a law that says you will punish anyone who treats anyone else as more important than you."

"Good idea," said the king.

"Say that anyone who disobeys will be thrown into a pit of lions," said the men.

"Good idea," said the king.

Daniel knew that everything was going wrong.

He still did what he believed was right. He still said prayers to God. He still obeyed God.

The men came to spy on him. They saw what he was doing.

Then they went and told the king.

"Daniel is praying to his God. He thinks his God is greater than you."

The king was sad. Now he must punish Daniel.

Daniel was
thrown into a pit
of hungry lions.

Everything was going wrong.

Daniel still did what he
believed was right.

He still said prayers to God.

He still obeyed God.

The next morning, the
king came to see what
had happened.

Daniel was alive. God had
not let the lions hurt
him.

"Hooray!" said the king. "I shall make a law that everyone must respect Daniel's God. He will be safe, and those bad men will be punished."

Everything was going right, and Daniel still did what he believed was right.

Nehemiah's Prayers

Nehemiah worked in the palace of the emperor of Persia. One day he was feeling sad.

"Why do you look so sad?" asked the emperor.

Nehemiah said a prayer to God. Then he answered, "My real homeland is far away. Our great city was knocked down in a fight. Now that the fight is over, my people want to go back and build it up."

The emperor let
Nehemiah go to help
mend the city—
the great city of
Jerusalem, in the
homeland of
the great-great-
great-ever-so-
many-great-
grandchildren
of Abraham.

Nehemiah rode
around the city on a
donkey, looking at
the broken walls.

Then he met with all the people.

"God has helped me get here," he said. "I want to help mend the city."

"Let's all mend it," the people said.

Everybody worked,
and the walls
began to grow...

and grow...

Some other people came
to watch. "You'll
never mend a city
as broken down
as this," they
laughed.

Nehemiah said a prayer to God. Then
he spoke to the people. "Don't worry
about what others think," he said.

Next Nehemiah heard that some people were planning to spoil all the work.

"Don't be afraid," said Nehemiah. "God will help us."

He told half the people to keep on building. The other half kept watch with swords and spears—they were ready to protect the builders.

At last the work was done. Everyone came to a great meeting.

A priest read out the laws God had given Moses: "Love God most of all, and love others as you love yourself."

Then everyone said a prayer:

"God, you made the world.
You chose Abraham to be the
great-grandfather of our people.
You chose Moses to lead us to freedom.
You took us to a homeland.
You gave us good laws.
We have sometimes disobeyed you
and made everything go wrong.
We are sorry, and we promise now
to keep your laws."

Nehemiah was happy. God
had answered all his prayers.

Tell me the stories of Jesus
  I love to hear;
things I would ask him to tell
  me if he were here;
scenes by the wayside, tales
  of the sea,
stories of Jesus, tell them to me.

A children's hymn

New Testament

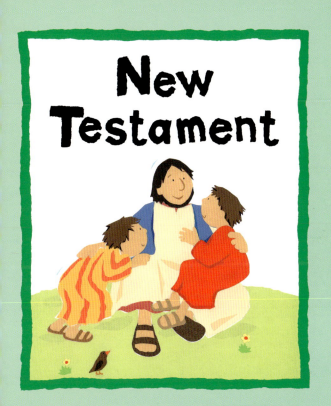

Baby Jesus

In the little town of Nazareth lived a young woman named Mary. She was looking forward to getting married.

One day, an angel came to visit her.

"Don't be afraid," said the angel.

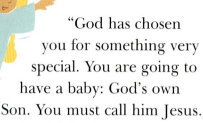

"God has chosen you for something very special. You are going to have a baby: God's own Son. You must call him Jesus. He will bring God's blessings to the world."

Mary was very surprised but she agreed. "I will do as God wants," she said.

Mary was looking forward to marrying Joseph. But when Joseph heard Mary's news, he was worried.

Then an angel spoke to him in a dream. "Take care of Mary," said the angel. "Her baby is God's own Son. He will bring God's blessings to all the world."

Joseph was very puzzled, but he said
he would take care of Mary.

And together they went to
take part in a great counting
of people that was being
done. They went to
Bethlehem.

The town was very
busy. The only place to
stay was in a room full
of animals.

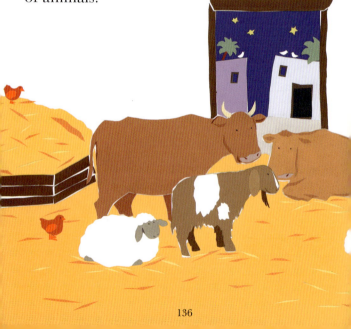

There, Mary's baby was born. Mary wrapped him in swaddling clothes. She laid him to sleep in a manger.

Out in the fields nearby, shepherds were watching their sheep. An angel appeared.

"Do not be afraid," said the angel. "Tonight, in Bethlehem, a baby has been born: God's special king, who will bring God's blessings to the world."

Then all the angels sang
together for joy.

The shepherds went to
Bethlehem.

They found Mary and the baby,
just as the angel had said.

Far away, wise men saw a special star
in the night sky.

"It is a sign that a new king has been
born," they said. "We must go and
find him."

The star led them to the place
where Jesus was.

They brought him gifts: gold,
frankincense and myrrh.

Mary smiled. The gifts for Jesus were
gifts for a king.

"The king who will bring God's
blessings to the world," she said to
herself.

Jesus Grows Up

Jesus grew up in Nazareth.

He learned the old
stories: about Noah
and Abraham and
many others.

He learned about Moses and the laws God had given him: "Love God most of all, and love others as you love yourself."

Every year, the people remembered the story of Moses and the great escape from Egypt. They held a special festival called Passover.

The best place to be at festival time was the big city of Jerusalem. When Jesus was twelve, he went with Mary and Joseph and lots of people from Nazareth.

The most important part of the festival took place in the Temple.

All around, wise teachers sat and
talked about the old stories and the
laws God had given Moses.

After the festival, everyone from
Nazareth set off for home.

They had gone some way when Mary
thought, "Where is Jesus? I haven't
seen him all day."

No one had seen him.

Mary and Joseph rushed
back to Jerusalem.

At last they found Jesus.
He was sitting with the wise
teachers, talking about the old
stories and the laws.

"Why are you here?" asked Mary. "We have been so worried about you."

"Why?" said Jesus. "Didn't you know that I had to be in my Father's house?"

Mary didn't really understand.
She just wanted Jesus to be safe.

Then Jesus went back home. He
grew to be a man. He was a good
son to his parents.
He learned the
kind of work
that Joseph did.

Then, one day, he went off
to begin a new kind of work.

Jesus became a wise teacher.
He helped people understand
the old stories and the laws.
He wanted people to
understand what God
is like.

He wanted people to know
how much God loves them.

Jesus and His Friends

Jesus the wise teacher told people about God. He told people that God loves them and welcomes them as friends.

"Follow me," said Jesus. "Come and listen to what I have to say, and help spread the news."

"We will come," said the fishermen. They left their fishing nets and their boat. They followed Jesus.

"I will come," said the tax collector. He left his money and his greedy friends to follow Jesus.

"I will come," said the rich lady, "for he is showing people the loving way to live, and I want to help."

There were other women,
too, who followed Jesus:
some rich and some poor.

"We will follow Jesus," said the mother and the father, "for our little girl was dead…"

"But Jesus made me as alive as can be," danced the little girl.

Other people danced too: people who had not been able to walk until Jesus made them well.

The sparrows
twittered happily
in the olive trees.

They swooped
close to Jesus.

They dared to hop
near his feet.

Something seemed to tell
them that Jesus noticed them
and loved them as well.

Some mothers came to Jesus. "We want Jesus to say a prayer for our children," they said.

"Sorry," said some of his
friends. "He's too busy."

"I am not too busy," said
Jesus. "I welcome children.
For God welcomes children.

"So all of my friends must welcome little children and love them."

The Hole in the Roof

Many people came to see Jesus and to listen to what he had to say. Some of the people were teachers. They were not all sure that they liked Jesus' teaching.

One day, Jesus was talking
to people inside a house.
It was very crowded.

Yet more people
came to see Jesus.

"We have heard he can heal people
by miracles," they said. "Our friend
cannot walk. We are carrying him
here on his sleeping mat so Jesus
can heal him."

There was a problem:
they could not even get
into the house.

On the outside of the house,
steps led up to the flat roof.

The men took their
friend up onto the roof.

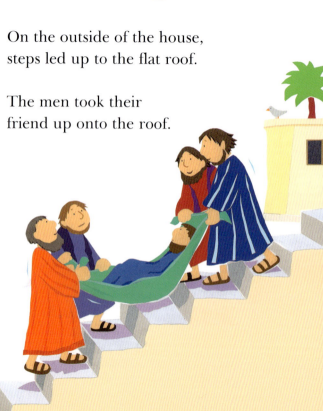

They made a hole in the roof
and let the man down on ropes,

right in front of Jesus.

"All the bad that is in you has
been forgiven," said Jesus with
a smile.

"He can't say that!" said some of the wise teachers to each other. "Only God can say that."

Jesus smiled. He wanted people to understand that God loves people, that God forgives people, that God wants to make people well, and that God wants to be friends with people.

He said to the man, "Get up and walk."

The man got up and
walked home. He even
carried his sleeping mat.

"God has done wonderful
things for me," he said to
his friends.

The Boat
in the Storm

Jesus was very busy. There
always seemed to be a lot of
people wanting to see him.

One evening, he said to his close friends, "Come, let's go in our boat across to the other side of the lake."

His friends got into the boat with him.

In the boat, Jesus soon fell
asleep.

Suddenly a strong wind began
to blow.

The waves began to crash
against the sides of the boat.

The waves began to
spill into the boat.

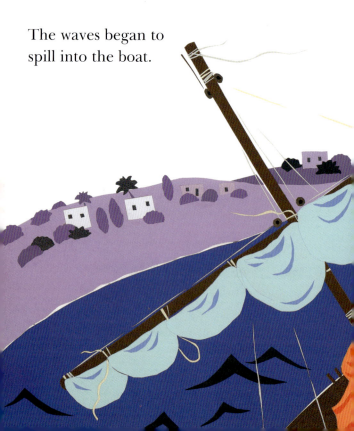

"Wake up and help us," shouted Jesus' friends. "We are going to sink with the boat!"

185

Jesus stood up.

"Be quiet," he said to the waves.
"Be still," he said to the wind.

Then everything was calm.
Everything that was dark
and dangerous and scary
just went away.

The day came, bright and
clear.

"What made you so scared?"
asked Jesus. "Don't you believe
in God?"

Jesus' friends knew they were
safe, but they were more
scared than ever.

"Who is our friend Jesus?"
they asked each other. "Who
can he be? Even the wind and
waves obey him."

The Good Samaritan

A teacher once came and asked Jesus a question: "What is the right way to live?"

Jesus asked him a question: "You are a teacher. What do the old stories and the laws say?"

'Love God most of all, and love others as you love yourself," answered the man.

'You are right," said Jesus. 'You know what to do."

'But who are these 'others'?" asked the man.

Jesus told a story.

"Once there was a man who went on a journey.

"On the way, robbers attacked him. They took everything he had and beat him up.

"They left him lying in the road.

"A priest from the Temple came along.

"He saw the man, but hurried on by on the other side of the road.

"A helper from the Temple
came along.

"He came and looked
at the man. Then he
hurried on by.

"A Samaritan came along."

"Samaritans are no good," said someone listening. "They don't like us, and we don't like them."

Jesus went on with the story:
"The Samaritan saw the
man. He stopped. He
bandaged the man's cuts.

"Then he lifted the man onto
his donkey and took him to
an inn.

"He gave the innkeeper some money. 'Take care of him till I come back,' he said. 'If you need to spend more, I'll pay the extra.'"

Then Jesus asked the teacher a question: "Who showed the right way to love others?"

"The one who was kind," answered the teacher.

Jesus said, "You go, then,
and do the same."

The Lost Sheep

Jesus welcomed all kinds of people: he didn't seem to mind what sort of people they were.

Some had become rich by cheating.

Some lived bad lives.

Some had the kinds of diseases that no one else wanted to get near.

The teachers were surprised. "What sort of person is Jesus if he wants to be friends with them?" they wondered.

Jesus told a story.

"Imagine that you have a hundred sheep. You take good care of them.

"One day when you are
counting them, you find
that one is missing.

"Where can it be?
What are you going to do?

"You leave the other ninety-nine nibbling in the pasture.

"You go looking for the one that is lost.

"You look high...

and low...

and everywhere in between...

"When you find it, you are
so happy you pick it up and
carry it home.

"You call out to your friends,
'Come and celebrate with me!
I had lost this sheep, but I
have found it again!'

"God is like that shepherd," said Jesus. "God sees the people who live good lives. God also sees those who have wandered away from what is good—and God cares about them too.

"There is more happiness in heaven when one is found and brought back home than over ninety-nine that are already safe."

A Prayer for Always

Jesus liked to pray to God.

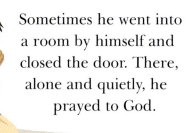

Sometimes he went into a room by himself and closed the door. There, alone and quietly, he prayed to God.

Sometimes he got up early and went for a walk in the hills. There, alone and quietly, he prayed to God.

"Teach us to pray," his
friends asked him.

"Here is a prayer for
always," said Jesus.

"Father in heaven:
May your name be kept holy.
May your Kingdom come
and may your will be done
on earth as it is in heaven."

"I know what that means,"
said one of the friends.
"God is our kind father. We
want people to obey God so
the whole world is as good
as heaven."

"Next," said Jesus, "say this:

"Give us today the food
we need."

"Oh good, I don't like being
hungry," said one.

"Food makes the body strong," said another, "but we also need God to encourage us, to make us strong inside."

That made everyone think.

"Ask God this," said Jesus.

"Forgive us the wrongs we have done, as we forgive the wrongs that others have done to us."

"Do we always have to forgive everyone?" asked the friend called Peter. "I try, but some people go on doing bad things."

"You must forgive everyone over and over again," said Jesus.

"Then," said Jesus, "say this:

"Do not bring us to hard testing, but keep us safe from the Evil One."

Everyone looked a bit sad.

"Do hard things happen to people who live as God wants?" someone asked.

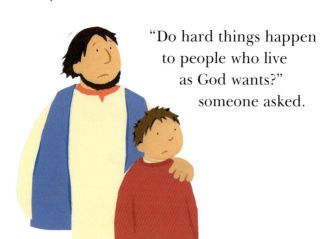

Jesus sighed and nodded. He knew there were hard times ahead.

"But God is God forever and ever," another replied.

And that made everyone glad.

Almost the End

It was a day in spring, on the road to Jerusalem.

Many people were going to celebrate the Passover festival at the Temple there.

Jesus came along, riding on a donkey.

The crowds welcomed him like a king. They waved palm branches and cheered. "This must be the beginning of Jesus making the whole world a better place," they said to each other.

Jesus went to the Temple. It was like a marketplace. People were selling the things people needed to buy for the festival.

Jesus could see that they were
making people pay too much.

Suddenly he began upsetting
the whole market.

"How dare you!" shouted the people in
charge of the Temple.

"The Temple is meant to be a place where you pray," said Jesus. "Not a place where people are cheated."

The people in charge were very angry.

"We must get rid of Jesus," they whispered. They began to make a plan.

A few days later, Jesus met with his
friends to eat the festival meal.

He warned them of hard times ahead.

He told them always to love one
another.

He shared bread and wine with them.
He told them always to share bread
and wine and to remember him in
this special way.

Then Jesus went out to
a quiet place to pray.

"Father God," he said,
"I don't want these hard
times, but I will do what
you want."

Already one of Jesus' friends
had joined the plan to get rid
of Jesus.

He came with soldiers who
took Jesus away.

The next day, Jesus was put to death, nailed to a cross of wood.

In the evening, a few friends came and took the body to a tomb.

"We must say goodbye," said one.

The sky was getting dark. "This must be the end of Jesus making the world a better place," they wept.

Good News

It was the weekly day of rest. Jesus' friends were very sad, for Jesus was dead.

"We'll have to hide," said some. "We might get into trouble for being his friends."

"But we will go back to the tomb," said the women, "to say goodbye properly."

The next morning, very early, the women went. To their surprise, the tomb was open.

Inside were two angels in shining white clothes. "Jesus is not here," they said. "He is alive."

They ran to tell the others, but
no one really believed them.

That evening, two of Jesus' friends left Jerusalem for home. A man was going the same way. As they walked, they talked about Jesus.

"Stay with us," said the two friends when they reached home.

When they began the meal, the man said the mealtime prayer and broke the bread to share it.

The two friends gasped. It was Jesus.
But all at once he was gone.

Other friends saw Jesus.

He shared a meal with them.

He helped them understand
that God is a friend when
people face hard times, and
that God can make everything
good and right again.

He gave them a job to do—to
tell this news to all the world.

Soon after, Jesus went to heaven.

But God gave his friends the help they needed.

They suddenly felt brave.
They knew what to say.

They began to speak to
anyone who would listen.

"Jesus came to us from God," they explained.

"He came to tell us how much God loves us. People tried to stop him, but their plan hasn't worked.

"Jesus is alive, proving that his message is true: God wants everyone to give up bad ways and come home to a place of goodness. God welcomes us all as friends.

"That's everyone in the whole wide world forever."

The news has been spreading ever since.

Index

When you look up the pages in this list, remember to read the whole story to find out more.

to

from

Written and compiled by Lois Rock
Illustrations copyright © 2003
Alex Ayliffe
This edition copyright © 2011
Lion Hudson

The moral rights of the author and
illustrator have been asserted

A Lion Children's Book
an imprint of
Lion Hudson plc
Wilkinson House,
Jordan Hill Road,
Oxford OX2 8DR, England
www.lionhudson.com
ISBN 978 0 7459 6186 6

First edition 2003
This edition 2011
10 9 8 7 6 5 4 3 2 1 0

Acknowledgments
All unattributed prayers by Lois
Rock, copyright © Lion Hudson,
except the Lord's Prayer on page 116.
Prayers by Christina Goodings, Mark
Robinson and Sophie Piper copyright
© Lion Hudson. The Lord's Prayer
© English Language Liturgical
Consultation (ELLC), 1988, and used
by permission.
See: www.englishtexts.org

A catalogue record for this book is
available from the British Library

Typeset in 18/28 Baskerville BT
Printed in China September 2011
(manufacturer LH06)

my very first
Prayers

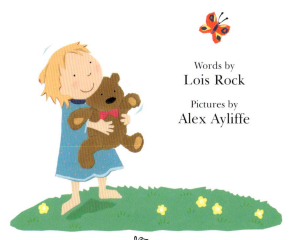

Words by
Lois Rock

Pictures by
Alex Ayliffe

LION
CHILDREN'S

Contents

morning

Dearest God,
on this new day,
listen to me
as I pray.

Dearest God,
the day is new:
help me in
the things I do.

7

Make all the bedclothes
neat for the day.
Fold the pyjamas,
put them away.
Open the curtains,
look to the light.
May this new day
be filled with delight.

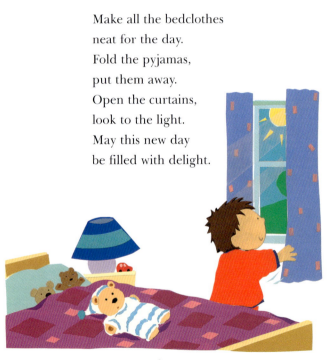

8

Who made the sun?
Who made the day?
Who made the hours
for work and play?

God made them all,
God made them good,
God helps us live
the way we should.

I wake
I wash
I dress
I say:

'Thank you
God
for this
new day.'

I lift my hands to the golden sun:
A shining day has just begun.
I wave my hand to heaven above:
May God protect me with his love.

O God,
May today be a good day.

May I think something good.
May I say something good.
May I learn something good.
May I make something good.
May I do something good.

May today be a good day,
O God.

This is a day for walking tall
This is a day for feeling small
This is a day for lots of noise
This is a day for quiet toys
This is a day to shout and sing
This is a day for everything.

Dear God,
Your sky is so big
and I am so small.
Never forget me,
never at all.

Dear God,
Please be my special friend:
closer than a hug,
softer than a quilt,
braver than a teddy bear.

Thank you, God in heaven,
For a day begun.
Thank you for the breezes,
Thank you for the sun.
For this time of gladness,
For our work and play,
Thank you, God in heaven,
For another day.

Traditional

me

God, look down from heaven:
Here on earth you'll see
Someone looking upwards –
That someone is me.

Bless my hair and bless my toes
Bless my ears and bless my nose
Bless my eyes and bless each hand
Bless the feet on which I stand
Bless my elbows, bless each knee:
God bless every part of me.

I look in the mirror and what do I see?
Someone who looks exactly like me!
I go out exploring but I haven't met
Anyone even a bit like me yet.

Dear God,
They say everyone's special,
As special as special can be.
But inside I just feel normal –
Is everyone special but me?

Dear God,
There is only one me.
I like what I like.
I don't like what I don't like.
I think what I think.
I do what I do.
I'm the only one of me you've got.
Please take care of me.

Happy, sulky, smiling, sad
Often good and sometimes bad
Through these ever-changing moods
Help me, God, to grow up good.

Dear God,

Please love me when I've been good.

Please love me when I've been bad.

Please love me when I've been ordinary.

Dear God,
Please help me to be really me
when I am with my family.

Help me to be really me
when I am with my friends.

Help me to be really me
when I am all by myself.

Dear God,
Some people forget my name.
Some people muddle my name.
Please will you remember my name
And remember me.

God, who made the earth,
The air, the sky, the sea,
Who gave the light its birth,
Careth for me.

God, who made the grass,
The flower, the fruit, the tree,
The day and night to pass,
Careth for me.

Sarah Betts Rhodes

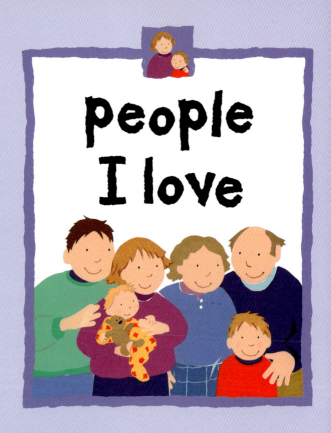

people
I love

God bless all those that I love;
God bless all those that love me;
God bless all those that love those
   that I love,
And all those that love those that
   love me.

New England sampler

Dear God,
When my mum is happy,
Let us laugh and play together.

When my mum is busy,
Let us do the work together.

When my mum is worried,
Let us sort things out together.

When my mum is weary,
Let us sit and rest together.

Dear God,
May my dad grow stronger and
wiser and funnier and cleverer.

Dear God,
May my mum grow stronger and
wiser and funnier and cleverer.

Dear God,
When I am with my mum and dad,
help me to take care of them.

When I am not with my mum and dad,
please take care of them for me
and bring us safely together again.

Grans are good
and grans are fun.
Let us love them –
every one.

God bless Grandad
through the bright blue day.
God bless Grandad
through the dark grey night.
God bless Grandad
when we hug together.
God bless Grandad
when we're out of sight.

I say a prayer for Baby –
'God help you and God bless,
God guard you and God guide you
With love and gentleness.'

Dear God,
Please love me
Love my sister
Love my brother.

Dear God,
Please take care of me
Take care of my sister
Take care of my brother.

Dear God,
Please bless me
Bless my sister
Bless my brother.

Thank you, dear God,
for the many kind people
who help us along our way,
who smile when we're happy,
who care when we're tearful,
who keep us safe all through the day.

Dear God,
Help me to be kind and gentle, friendly
and respectful to everyone I meet.

at home

Bless the window
Bless the door
Bless the ceiling
Bless the floor
Bless this place which is our home
Bless us as we go and come.

When the weather is cold
May our home be warm.

When the weather is wet
May our home be dry.

When the sun shines hot
May our home give shade.

When the world is dark
May our home be bright.

Let us take a moment
To thank God for our food,
For friends around the table
And everything that's good.

Knife and fork
and plate and spoon –
May the meal
be here soon.

Spoon and plate
and fork and knife –
Thank you, God,
who gives us life.

The Lord is good to me,
And so I thank the Lord
For giving me the things I need,
The sun, the rain, the appleseed.
The Lord is good to me.

Attributed to John Chapman,
planter of orchards

For health and strength
and daily food,
we praise your name,
O Lord.

Traditional

Underwear everywhere
Shoes in twos
So many clothes
I just can't choose.

So many clothes
I know I'm blessed
But oh – it's so hard
To get dressed.

The room is almost tidy
The toys are put away
I take a quiet moment
To thank God for the day.

Thank you, God, for all things cuddly
In a heap that's soft and muddly
Where I can lie down and rest
Like a dormouse in its nest.

things
I do

God, can you hear me?
This is my prayer:
Please take good care of me
Everywhere.

Dear God,
Teach me to be patient
so I can learn new things
one step at a time.

Dear God,
I think I've learned to walk,
Please help me learn to run,
And can you teach me somersaults?
They look like so much fun.

May my hands be helping hands
For all that must be done
That fetch and carry, lift and hold
And make the hard jobs fun.

May my hands be clever hands
In all I make and do
With sand and dough and clay and things
With paper, paint and glue.

May my hands be gentle hands
And may I never dare
To poke and prod and hurt and harm
But touch with love and care.

Words can make us happy
Words can make us sad
Words can leave us feeling calm
WORDS CAN MAKE US MAD!
So we must be careful
In the things we say
Dear God, help us choose the words
That we use today.

Let us build our friendships carefully
And if we should fall out and argue
Let us build our friendships carefully again.

Dear God,
Please help me learn to say, 'I'm sorry.'
Please help me learn to say, 'I forgive.'

When I am in a temper
When I get really mad
I can be very dangerous
I can be very bad.

I'm wild as a tiger
I'm wild as a bear
I'm wilder than a wildebeest
And I don't even care.

Dear God, who made the tiger,
Dear God, who made the bear,
Please let me know you love me still
And that you'll always care.

Mark Robinson

We give thanks
for all the things that are our very own.

We give thanks
for all the things that are ours to share.

We give thanks
for all the things that others share with us.

We give thanks
for all the things we can enjoy together.

God take care of everyone
Until we meet again
Keep us safe through sun and snow
And wind and hail and rain.

Out and about
And feeling small
God, please help me
If I fall.

Out and about
And walking tall
Trusting God
Not scared at all.

May God be watching over us
when we go out bravely.
May God be watching over us
so we come back safely.

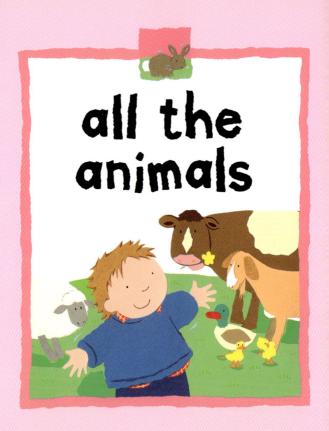

all the animals

All things bright and beautiful,
All creatures great and small,
All things wise and wonderful,
The Lord God made them all.

Mrs C.F. Alexander

The little bugs that scurry,
The little beasts that creep
Among the grasses and the weeds
And where the leaves are deep:
All of them were made by God
As part of God's design.
Remember that the world is theirs,
Not only yours and mine.

Dear God,
Please show extra kindness and love
to worms and snails and snakes and
frogs and everything strange and
slimy. Help us not to frighten them
even if they frighten us.

May the creatures of the wood
Live together as they should.

Dear God,
Thank you for the farmers
who work so hard to keep
their animals healthy and happy.

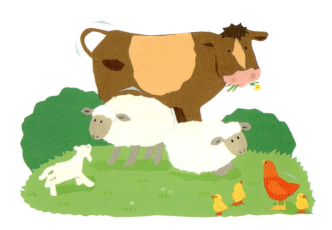

Dear God,
We hear cows mooing
and are glad for the milk they give us.

We hear sheep bleating
and are glad for the wool they give us.

We hear hens clucking
and are glad for the eggs they give us.

We hear all the sounds of the farmyard
and give thanks for the animals.

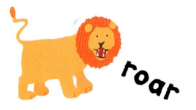

growl

Bless the hungry lion and its ROAR
Bless the big brown bear and its GROWL
Bless the sly hyena and its scary HA HA HA
Bless the wolves who see the moon and HOWL!

ha ha ha

howl

Multicoloured animals
With stripes and dots and patches:
God made each one different –
There isn't one that matches.

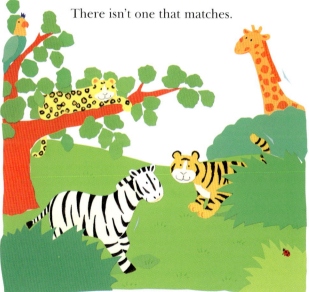

Dear God,
May our dog be loyal and
obedient and patient and gentle
and kind and fun. May everyone
in the family learn to be like that.

Dear God,

Please bless the cat.

Make it wild enough to be a great explorer.

Make it tame enough to come back home.

When little creatures die
And it's time to say goodbye
To a bright-eyed furry friend,
We know that God above
Will remember them with love:
A love that will never end.

If you have heard
the sound of birdsong
in the morning air,
then you will know
that heaven's music
reaches everywhere.

great
big world

Planet home,
our planet earth:
you have cradled us from birth.

Planet earth,
our planet home:
you were made by God alone.

Thank you, dear God,

For the good earth:
I stand upon it.

For the clean air:
I can breathe it.

For the pure water:
I can drink it.

For the fiery sun:
It warms the good earth.

Sunrise, moonrise,
Day and night:
Thank you, God,
For dark and light.

O God,
Keep the oceans and the seas
   where they belong,
Keep the rains and rivers
   where they belong,
Keep the highlands and the
   lowlands where they belong,
So that all your creatures may have
   a safe place to make their home.

Lord of the ocean,
Lord of the sea:
Let the fish swim
Strong and free.

Lord of the wavetops,
Lord of the shore:
Keep them safe
For evermore.

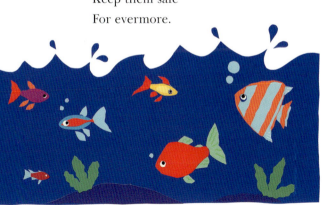

The trees grow down,
down into the earth,
right down into long ago.

The trees grow up,
up into the sky,
right up where the strong winds blow.

The trees, they sway,
they sway in the wind
and whisper a secret song:

'We thank you, God,
for keeping us safe,
that we might grow tall and strong.'

For sun
and for showers,
for seeds
and for flowers,
we give you thanks,
O God.

Angels spend the sunshine hours
Opening the summer flowers.
At the coming of the night
They come back to close them tight.

The morning clouds are orange and pink
As the sun climbs into the sky,
And white clouds drift in the faraway blue
At noon when the sun is high.
The sunset mixes up purple and mauve
With violet, gold and red,
And angels watch over me through the dark
When I'm asleep in my bed.

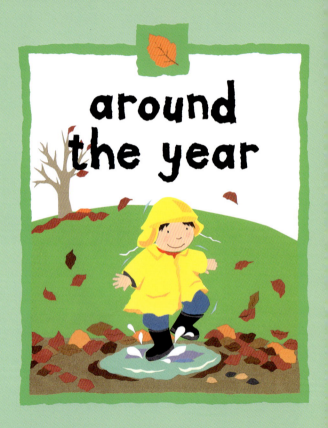

around the year

May the rain fall softly:
no flooding.
May the wind blow gently:
no storm.
May the sun shine brightly:
no burning.
May the weather be kindly
and warm.

God is waking the world again
Cold and frost are going.

God is waking the world again
New green leaves are growing.

God is waking the world again
Warmer winds are blowing.

God is waking the world again
Springtime flowers are showing.

Yesterday
I liked the rain,
But, dear God,
Please, not again!

Out of doors in the summer
Out of doors in the sun
Thank you, God, for the summer
And all of our outdoor fun.

A summertime place
of trees and flowers,
the gentle call of a dove,
the hum of a bee –
these things must be
a glimpse of heaven above.

Autumn berries
round and red:
by God's hand
the birds are fed.

Grey cloud, send your rain
to the green and growing grain.
White cloud, blow away
from the golden harvest day.

Winter boots for puddles
Winter boots for snow
Winter boots for all the muddy
   places that I go.

Winter hats for chilly days
Winter hats for storms
Thank you, God, for winter clothes
   that help to keep us warm.

The winter trees
are grey and bare.
God gives them
silver frost to wear.

Spring is green and yellow
and the summer, pink and gold.
Autumn's red soon turns to brown –
the year is getting old.
Wintertime is blue and white –
the ice is crystal clear:
All the colours dance around
the circle of the year.

quiet times

I'm standing here upon the earth
and looking to the sky.
I'm trusting that my quiet prayers
can reach to God on high.

Dear God,
Are you very grand?
Are you very holy?
Am I allowed to come near?

For I am not at all grand.
I don't really understand holy.
But I feel your love all around me.

Dear God,
Help me to grow up good,
and show me the way I
should go, so that I may
come at last to heaven and
already feel at home there.

I'm sitting
and thinking
and wondering
and wishing
and dreaming
and hoping
and praying

and hoping
and dreaming
and truly
believing
that God
can hear all
that I'm saying.

Dear God,
I am asking in my prayers:
May I receive all you want to give me.

Dear God,
I am seeking for you in my life:
May I find you and learn how to live
as your friend.

Dear God,
I am knocking on the door of heaven:
Open the door to your heavenly
home, where I may live as your
friend for ever.

Based on Matthew, chapter 7, verses 7–8

Dear God,
Please hear my prayers,
even when I cannot think
of the right words to say.

Dear God,
I am a brave explorer
in the world you have made.
Help me to make great discoveries
and to grow wise.

Dear God,
Everything I see in the world tells
me that there must be a Maker,
and I believe that Maker is you.

Our Father in heaven,
hallowed be your name,
your kingdom come,
your will be done,
on earth as in heaven.
Give us today our daily bread.
Forgive us our sins
as we forgive those who sin against us.
Lead us not into temptation
but deliver us from evil.
For the kingdom, the power,
and the glory are yours
now and for ever.
Amen.

make everything better

Dear God, I believe in goodness:
I believe it is stronger than badness.

Dear God, I believe in happiness:
I believe it is stronger than sadness.

Dear God,
May your good world
take care of us.
May we take care
of your good world.

Dear God,
When a perfect day
is spoiled,
help us find a way
to mend it.

Deeply gloomy
Deeply sad
When the day
Goes deeply bad.

Deeply hoping
God above
Will enfold me
In his love.

We say goodbye,
knowing that God loves me
and God loves you.

We say goodbye,
knowing that God will remember me
and God will remember you.

We say goodbye,
knowing that God will take care of me
and God will take care of you.

Dear God,
When things end in tears,
give us joyful beginnings.

Dear God,
I am feeling poorly –
wrap me in softness.

Dear God,
I am feeling poorly –
wrap me in cosiness.

Dear God,
I am feeling poorly –
wrap me in sleepiness.

Dear God,
Let me feel sleepy
and dream in happiness.

Dear God,
We think of those who are sick
and ask you to make them well.

Whenever there's something to share,
Help me to learn to be fair.

Heal the world's sorrows
Dry the world's tears
Calm the world's worries
End the world's fears.

Dear God,
May all the children of the world
have all they need
to grow up well
and to grow up happy.

special days

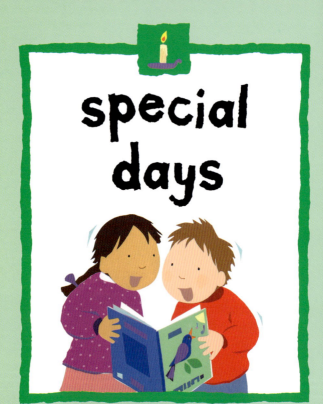

For each new year
and all it brings,
we give you thanks,
O God.

I count the days to Christmas
and I watch the evening sky.
I want to see the angels
as to Bethlehem they fly.

I'm watching for the wise men
and the royal shining star.
Please may I travel with them?
Is the stable very far?

I count the days to Christmas
as we shop and bake and clean.
The lights and tinsel sparkle,
and yet deep inside I dream

that as we tell the story
of Lord Jesus and his birth,
the things of everyday will fade
as heaven comes to earth.

A prayer for Advent

Away in a manger, no crib for a bed,
The little Lord Jesus laid down his sweet head.
The stars in the bright sky looked down where he lay,
The little Lord Jesus asleep on the hay.

The cattle are lowing, the baby awakes,
But little Lord Jesus, no crying he makes.
I love thee, Lord Jesus! Look down from the sky,
And stay by my side until morning is nigh.

Be near me, Lord Jesus, I ask thee to stay
Close by me for ever, and love me, I pray.
Bless all the dear children in thy tender care,
And fit us for heaven, to live with thee there.

A traditional Christmas carol

There is a green hill far away,
Outside a city wall,
Where the dear Lord was crucified
Who died to save us all.

He died that we might be forgiven,
He died to make us good;
That we might go at last to heaven,
Saved by his precious blood.

A traditional Good Friday song with
words by Mrs C.F. Alexander

In the Easter garden
the leaves are turning green;
in the Easter garden
the risen Lord is seen.

In the Easter garden
we know that God above
brings us all to heaven
through Jesus and his love.

Seed and shoot and ear and grain
Growing in the sun and rain.
Grain and flour and dough and bread –
By God's harvest we are fed.

A harvest prayer

The apple-tree blossom was pink and white
The summertime fruits were green
But now the apples of red and gold
Are much too much for the tree to hold:
God's harvest blessings are seen.

A harvest prayer

Dear God,
When the darkness makes us feel
afraid, bring us safely into the
light of your goodness and love.

A prayer for All Saints' Eve

Dear God,
We think of the people
we know today
who help us
to follow Jesus.

We think of the people
from days gone by
whose stories help us
to follow Jesus.

We think of their wise words
and their good deeds
and ask you to help us
to follow Jesus.

A prayer for All Saints' Day

now the day is over

Tucked up in my little bed,
I say a little prayer
For all the people in this house
And people everywhere.

Sophie Piper

Hands together, close your eyes,
Pray to God above
That the night be filled with peace,
And the day with love.

Sophie Piper

Now I lay me down to sleep,
I pray thee, Lord, thy child to keep;
Thy love to guard me through the night
And wake me in the morning light.

Traditional

Kindly Jesus, lead me
as a shepherd leads the sheep
to the greenest pastures
and the quiet waters deep.
Guard me from all dangers
and the fear that haunts the night.
In your goodness, bring me safely
into heaven's light.

The moon shines bright,
The stars give light
Before the break of day;
God bless you all,
Both great and small,
And send a joyful day.

Traditional

I see the moon,
And the moon sees me:
God bless the moon,
And God bless me.

Traditional

The angel of dreams
  is dressed in blue –
A dream for me
  and a dream for you.

The angel of dreams
  is dressed in pink –
And softly into
  your bed you sink.

The angel of dreams
  is dressed in white –
The day is done
  and so goodnight.

Sophie Piper

Clouds in the sky above,
Waves on the sea,
Angels up in heaven
Watching over you and me.

Christina Goodings

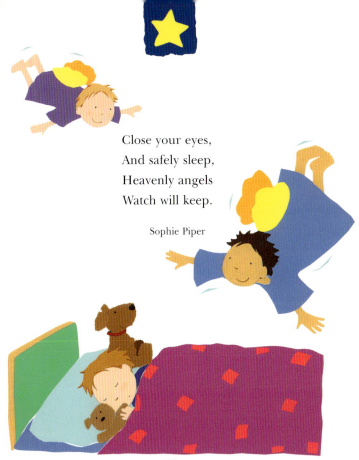

Close your eyes,
And safely sleep,
Heavenly angels
Watch will keep.

Sophie Piper

first lines